PAUL UCCUSIC · BEE MEDICINE

This book "bee medicine" is also available in following languages:

german
arabic
finnish

Paul Uccusic

BEE MEDICINE

**The healing virtues of pollen,
royal jelly and propolis
and their applications.
With the latest
research.**

FACULTAS

Paul Uccusic · Doctor Bee

This edition published 1982 for Newman Turner
Publications Limited, Unit 18, Goldsworth Park Trading
Estate, Woking, Surrey GU21 3BJ, by
Facultas, Publishers for medicine and pharmacology,
Berggasse 4, A-1090 Vienna, Austria.
Copyright text – Paul Uccusic 1981
Reader: Maurice Hanssen

ISBN 3 7205 1225 8

Phototypeset by Alfabetstudio, Vienna
Printed in Austria by Wograndl, Mattersburg

CONTENTS

And the Lord spoke to the bee: "Seek housing in the mountains and in the trees and in that which they (mankind) have erected. And then eat of all fruits and take to the comfortable path of your Lord". From their bodies comes a potion of differing colour in which is medication for man. See, herein is a sign for reflective people.

Koran, 16th Sure, 70-71

Preface

The bee has existed for more than 30 million years. It is surprising that it has retained its structure unchanged for so long.

Therefore, it must be harmonic, or in the language of our present age, optimal.

Nobody knows if the bee's nature determines it to be a friend of man, that is to say, whether that which it does is done for man.

Anyway, it does it.

Therefore I have written this book.

I thank not only the bees but also many people, researchers, bee-keepers, doctors and poets, who have occupied themselves with bees.

It is impossible to name them all.

Only two of them: Paul Urban and Mitja Vošnjak, who taught me to see the secrets of the bee-hive . . .

Vienna, August 1981

PAUL UCCUSIC

CHAPTER 1

Healing harmony

The population explosion, rapid industrialisation and the overemphasis on the material aspects of the world have made living space, raw materials, energy and capital scarce. Harmony and quiet have become such rarities that people often sacrifice everything to obtain them.

We have too many sources of the quantity of life but less and less of the quality of life.

A reliable indicator for this world-wide crisis is the condition of our health.

Do not let me be misunderstood; Illness is a part of human existence, just as eating and breathing, birth and death. But it is very thought-provoking that, to mention only one example, the investment of many billions of dollars and the work of specialists for decades in the war against cancer, the scourge of mankind, has led to nothing other than to a statement of resignation· Everything senselessly blown to the wind, not a single major step forward achieved. In the future everything will be left to the individual initiative of gifted researchers.

Never before in the history of mankind were so many people chronically ill. Never before has so much capital and technology been invested in health systems, and never before was success so minimal.

In order to avoid my being misunderstood, I would agree that accident surgery and emergency medicine have become very efficient disciplines.

Science and technology have arrived in these branches at a reasonable systhesis. But nothing is done for the masses of the chronically ill. Or when it is, the wrong thing.

How is one supposed to become healthy within the mechanized and automated medicine of our times, which wants to know nothing at all about the soul and about the spirit, only that which it can measure with instruments. Within a system which is threatening to fail because of its own pretentiousness, because of its arrogant "I know better", because of the demands it taxes itself with, and because of its megalomania? Because of the hubris of him, who, blindly believing in progress, thinks everything is possible to the point that the gigantic hospitals, the wholebody scanners, the computer tomographs and the completely automatic diagnostic methods make him forget the one thing for which all of this was made – the human being.

As the physicians of old, Hippocrates, Galen, Hufeland, Paracelsus, Avicenna, Brauchle, Aschner and many others knew, health is more than having an undamaged body.

Health is the harmony of body, soul and spirit.

And right here is to be found the root of the failure of so called health systems of all the industrialized states; they judge a measure first according to its utility, and then as to whether or not it fits into the system. Whether or not it helps man or whether or not it is capable of harmonizing him, is of less interest.

But no ill person will be cured with medicine alone. Harmony will not be reached with the disharmonious bunches of disinterested managers, whose highest idol's name is Mammon.

A system in which, from the beginning, the picture of man is false, is not suited to restoring complete balance, health and harmony to a person.

It is only possible with nature.

These problems didn't just arise today. There have always been philosophers who were of the opinion that everything is attainable – in the Old Testament, in Aristotelian Greece and finally in the modern era of Descartes. The multi-facetted power of reason has always fascinated man.

But no epoch has been as totally captivated by this as ours.

It is not only that earlier there were more correctives, such as priests, prophets, Shamans and genuine doctors, but that also man's feeling of harmony, his knowledge of the second reality, of cosmic relationships were apparently less disturbed. Earlier, it was simple, in view of an undamaged nature, to recognize the fact that one can heal only *with nature*. Today's medical technocrats wage a "desperate war against nature", and they have no success!

But healing harmony exists, even though many of our medical people, who falsely call themselves physicians, do not recognize it.

This work is the result of decades of searching for this harmony, of searching for effectiveness and simplicity.

An attitiude of perpetual humility must be maintained: If efforts do not observe the essence of the point of time (the Greeks knew this principle well and called it Cairos), the essence of nature and the eternal laws of life, they are all in vain. This can be perfectly illustrated by the inspired words of Saint Hildegard von Bingen: "The ill person will become healthy, except when God does not wish it so".

Nothing can be added to such clarity.

This small book deals with three apparently insignificant things: pollen, royal jelly and propolis. All three are bee products.

But they are more than that.

They are the result of thousands of years of cooperation between plant and animal, between blossom and bee. They result from exactly that harmony, which is at work in all healing.

Strangely enough, nobody has been able to destroy this harmony with excessive technologies. There are certainly places in which industrial filth and automobile exhaust have encroached upon medicinal herbs and pollen, indeed, medicinal herbs have been turned into poisonous plants, as Maurice Mességué the great French natural healer has been able to prove. But the symbiosis of blossom and bee has remained intact outside the centres of concentrated population.

The healing power of plants (plants are always appropriate to their time and place as proved elsewhere [56, 61]*), which has always been held in high esteem by a few people, is not just doubled by the power of the bee but increased many times.

Natural scientists have found out what the reason for that effect is: It is because of the enzymes of the bee's organism.

But the bee-keepers knew that before them.

And this knowledge is ancient.

Honey is not where the plant-bee-healing principal is at its strongest – there it is at its weakest. Strengthened, it appears in pollen, in royal jelly (gelée royale) (the nutritive substance produced explicitly for the rearing of the egg-laying queen) and in the strange antibiotic, propolis a resin gathered from buds, with which the bees protect their hiro from infection. Experience has shown

* The numbers in brackets refer to the bibliography.

that certain combinations have a very special effectiveness.

Changing behavior

Here is a warning: Although so many and such spectacular cases of successful healing are recorded here, in this book, there is more to the fundamental harmonizing or an ill person than the swallowing of a Melbrosia capsule of the sucking of propolis chewing gum. I myself and dozens of people I know have experienced the power of this bee-blossom-harmony, but in more serious cases (today many are serious because they have been chronically ill for a long time) one preventive measure alone is too little. Natural medicine always prefers a polyvalent therapy, that is a treatment which deals with as many points of the sick organism as possible. Centres of infection have to be cleared up and a derailed metabolism corrected. The system's illness must be attacked at the roots.

Behaviour which causes illness must be *entirely* changed. Melbrosia is good for impotence, but a reasonable way of life (going to bed early, and avoiding the misuse of nicotine and alcohol) is better. And the best is a natural way of life *and* Melbrosia, so one harmonizing step is enhanced by the other.

A single example might make this clear.

Propolis is probably the only remedy that is effective for tennis elbow or radio-humeral epicondylitis. Around 80 percent of the epicondylites treated with propolis salve, respond – an extraordinarily high percentage. But of course, any straining of tendons and joints has to be avoided during the

11

period of application and afterwards (and many weeks may be necessary). He who swings his racket while still carrying a propolis compress, should not be surprised that his complaints are not disappearing . . . .

And he who has heard of the healing effect of propolis on gastric ulcers, but who continues to strain his digestive system with bacon, grilled chops and whisky can be certain that he has thoroughly misunderstood the healing principal of harmonization.

CHAPTER 2

Pollen – the key to fertility

Blossom-pollen is a world of its own.

Of the larger types there are 14.000 pollen grains per gramme, but there are kinds of pollen with far smaller grains, 300.000 of which are necessary to form one gramme.

Regardless of the fact, pollen is just about everywhere as people who suffer from hay fever know only too well! The meadows and forests of mountainous Austria produce many hundreds of thousands of tons each year! Yet pollen is valuable and expensive. It is calculated that a trained worker harvests no more than one kilogramme of the especially precious comb-pollen (perga-bee-bread) a day.

With the help of the bees, of course.

Pollen is the male principal of plants, it serves the fertilization of the female ovules. In ancient Assyria, in Egypt and among the Hebrews this was a known fact; the Assyrians had annual ceremonies in which the pollen of the male date palm was dusted onto the female trees.

Following the television series "Biene Maja" ("Maja Bee"), every Austrian child became aware that pollen serves the bee as food. Scientists have found out that 150.000 bees gain their nourishment each year from between 30 and 50 kilogrammes of pollen.

During the 1960's Soviet scientists have been pre-eminent in discovering that many of the people who are one hundred years old or older regularly ate honey combined with bee-bread (pollen which is fermented and made nonperishable by bees). Further research has shown that pollen contains all the substances needed for living: sugars, minerals, trace elements, fats aromatic substances, hormones, vitamins and amino acids (proteins).

The latter are especially important: Our life is based upon them, and it is certainly no coincidence that different kinds of pollen contain between 20 and 22 amino acids*.

It has been calculated that 100 grammes of pollen contain the same amount of amino acids as 500 grammes of beef or seven eggs, and furthermore, that about 30 grammes of pollen (two level teaspoons) is enough to cover the daily protein requirement of an adult. Thanks to the other components, it can be said that he, who nourishes himself for months with pollen alone, will never have deficiency symptoms – in contrast to all other forms of nutrition with individual substances.

The above – average incidence of pollen consumption among Soviet citizens, who are older than 100 (Professor N. Tsitsin's study, Moscow 1964), encourages not only the speculation that pollen is something like a geriatricum and a fountain of youth, but also natural medicine's opinion that the substances needed for living, exist in pollen in perfect distribution.

Even teaching doctors have at last arrived at the idea that the methods of ambitious chemists – whose desire is the isolation of active substances – is to be utilized only in the rarest of cases in human medicine. Naturally occuring combinations of active substances have, in most cases, a better

---

* These include: alanine arginine asparatic acid, cystine glutamic acid, glycine histidine hydroxyproline, leucine, isoleucine, lysine, methionine, phenylalanine, tryptophan, proline, serine, threonine, tyrosine, valine and more seldom, amino butyric acid.

effect on the ill organism than the pure substances isolated by pharmacy. Poppy seed concentrate, which is known as opium, has, for example, considerably fewer side – effects and is considerably less addictive than morphine, which is isolated from this concentrate. Morphine is a *single* substance, whereas opium is a mixture of at least 20 alkaloids with other natural substances of lesser effect.

An active substance isolated from pollen would be comparable to a single note without an echo, without accompaniment. In this comparison pollen is like a harmonious symphony.

Pollen as a sex-stimulus

Comparisons may be poetic, but in the scientific-thinking twentieth century they prove nothing. Nowadays statistically sound investigations are required and in medicine this is not done without a double-blind test. One group of patients receives the preparation to be tested, a second (control) group a tablet or ampoule without the effective substances, a so-called placebo. When the patient does not know if he has received the medicament or the placebo, we speak of a blind test. When not even the doctor knows, who received what, it is called a double-blind trial.

The Yugoslavian gynaecologist Dr. Izet Osmanagić conducted such a trial in the school of medicine at the university of Sarajevo in the years 1978 and 1979.

His basic idea was that the fertilization process of humans is rather similar to that of plants, and that therefore pollen could help in cases of barrenness. Why should the ancient Assyrian fertilization ritual not be applicable to tired, sexually disinterested, unfruitful and impotent men?

At his and neighbouring clinics, Osmanagić found 78 men, from whose marriage no children had been born and in which it was highly probable that the woman was not the "guilty" party. 38 of them received a mixture of pollen and gelée royale called *Melbrosia Executive* (of which the discoverer, Paul Urban claims that pollen and gelée royale together give rise to a synergistic effect, what is to say, they increase each other's effectiveness), the control group, also 38 men, received the placebo. Osmanagić notes in his publication that the administration of a placebo "is not ethically completely justifiable, because the patients who turn to us, do in fact, expect help", but he can console himself, because nevertheless, four of the men of the placebo group reported an improvement of their condition. No effective substances, just with "psychology" . . .

Medically two aspects are understood under "potency": the ability to perform the sexual act (potentia coeundi) and the procreative capacity (potentia generandi). A third is the desire (libido) and as a consequence of his investigations, Osmanagić became aware that these three are closely interrelated.

The sperm's condition is important for the procreative capacity. It depends on the number and the mobility of the sperm cells, and right at this point, much could be expected from the power of pollen. Because pollen contains a lot of fructose (fruit sugar), which serves the sperm cells as an energy donor, and also the amino acids arginine, histidine and glycine which are important for the production of sperms in the testicles. Similarly

16

effective are the growth agents (auxins) and the plant hormones (phytosterols) obtained from gelée royale.

The patients had to take two Melbrosia Executive capsules a day. And after only a few days it became apparent not only that the formerly tired men had turned into interested lovers but also that the number of sperm cells and their motility had increased. After 14 months of testing Osmanagić was able to register

5 very good
24 good, and
5 weak results

in the group of those who had received pollen and gelée royale.

Four patients had not appeared at the final check up. In the control group (placebo without effective substances) there were

0 very good
4 good and
28 weak results [35].

It has thus been proven, beyond reasonable doubt (85,3% rate of success with Melbrosia Executive) not only that pollen and gelée royale increase potency (hence, in connection with this, the improvement of the general physical and mental condition), that there was intercourse more often and that the quality and intensity of the sensations were improved, but also that in this combination they are capable of raising the number, strength and motility of the sperm cells.

In three cases the desired pregnancy appeared –

and this although these had been "second or third -
degree cases of oligoasthenospermia and long
lasting impotency before treatment" (Osmanagić).

(Oligoasthenospermia: too few and too weak
sperm cells.)

Of course, pollen and gelée royale do not only
help men.

CHAPTER 3

A friend of women

There are as many kinds of pollen as there are plants that bloom, but in practice it is difficult to separate, for instance, the horse chestnut's pollen (which, as other effective substances of this plant, helps relieve, specifically, venous ailments) from that of the pear (heart-restorative) or from that of the dandelion (with tonic effect on the liver, the bladder and the prostate gland). Bees swarm in their hive's surrounding and collect pollen from each blossoming plant. The result is therefore a mixture of many types of pollen.

Expierence has shown that certain types of pollen agree better with women.

Upon this basis of century-old knowledge, some gifted individuals have developed combinations of effective substances.

Through skillful selection of some types of pollen, *Melbrosia p.l.d.* – Melbrosia pour les dames, that is a preparation for women – has been formed from the *Melbrosia Executive* mentioned in the previous chapter, which is actually intended for men. Of course, the producers assure us, *Melbrosia Executive* can be taken by women just as *Melbrosia p.l.d.* by men, but the latter reaches its full spectrum of effectiveness only with women.

Because they have their own problems.

Let us examine the point where a young girl enters sexual maturity – the time to get to know a new hormonal situation. Under the pressure of hard work at school, her period is not on time as it should be.

Or when it does come, it is extremly painful.

Later there is the burden of a career, or that of a household with children; often there is the double-load, household – career. It is important, especially for the employed woman, not only to have strength and to look good, but also to develop mental resistance.

It is the hormonal occurrences at a mature age which start to play havoc with the woman's body. The change, menopause, can last years under certain circumstances, with its weight and figure problems, and also with its blood pressure complaints, flushes and headaches. Here, qualified help is highly appreciated. And it is very important that medicaments be easily tolerated and have no side-effects because they may have to be taken over a period of years.

Gelée royale and the resin propolis, deliver in all the above mentioned cases the desired aid completely without side-effects. The gynaecologist, Professor Izet Osmanagić, of whom we have already spoken, has also conducted many investigations in this area.

A capsule under the tongue

As a treatment of extremely painful menstruation, mostly with accompanying headaches, nausea, vomiting, fainting and weakness or of outright infantility (underdevelopment of the uterus and other female organs), 23 young women between the age of 18 and 22 received daily a capsule of Melbrosia for 60 days at Osmanagić's clinic.

For greater effectiveness, the capsule is taken sublingually, that is, the capsule is laid under the tongue where it melts, or the contents emptied and placed under the tongue. At the end of the treatment period, six (21,1%) of the patients were completely relieved of pain and the pain of another 12 (52,2%) had been reduced to the extent that Osmanagić was able to describe the results as "good". There was only slight improvement with three (13,1%) of the women, none what ever with two (8,6%). Because of incombatability, one woman had to leave the treatment right at the start.

If the "very good" and "good" results are calculated, those being the ones in which a clear, definite effect of the pollen and gelée royale preparation was observed, the sum is a proud 78,3%!

Colloquially expressed, more than three quarters of the patients treated with Melbrosia were helped by this method.

Dr. Bogdan Tekavčić of the gynaecological clinic in Ljubljana, Yugoslavia, reports similar results. He conducted a double-blind test with two groups, each consisting of 30 young women between the age of 18 and 22, some of them were suffering from asthenia (weakness, inability to gain weight), and all of whom from irregular and painful menstruation. 30 young women received a Melbrosin capsule for a period of two months, the 30 in the second group, one which looked the same but without effective contents.

After the two months, Tekavčić checked his results: In Ljubljana too, the power of the bee preparation was quite apparent:

● 11 of the especially weak women had gained between one and three kilogrammes. Weight-gaining percentage 78,5, which is highly significant!

● 12 out of 14 women treated were relieved from their menstrual pains either completely or considerably, that is 85,7%.
That is also highly significant! It is to be particularly stressed that most of the complaints had already disappeared after just a month's treatment.

And what did the "success" of the control group look like, that is to say, that of those young women who had received capsules without effective elements (placebo)? Only two out of 13 patients gained weight (15,3%, insignificant) and only three out of 13 (23%, also insignificant) were relieved of their menstrual complaints [52].

A living tradition

At this point a word is necessary as to why scientific works from Yogoslavia, the Soviet Union and other Eastern-block Countries are so often mentioned here.

The main reason is that bees and bee-products have had their place in nutrition and folk medicine in the Balkan countries, in Poland, Czechoslovakia and the Soviet Union for centuries. Many states have indeed more than a few research institutes in this field. One of the most famous is the Apimondia Institute in Bucharest and the Rumanians are proud that "their" bees have been serving mankind for millenia.

There are other institutes in Yugoslavia and in the Soviet Union, in Poland and in Czechoslovakia; dozens of scientists deal with "Dr. Bee". For many, but not ultimately for political and economic reasons, the potent Western pharmaceutical industry has not been able to establish itself in the Eastern states. The tradition of natural medicine has stayed alive more in the East than in the West and one of its most important branches is apiarian medicine. There are, of course, researchers in the U.S.A., who are interested in bees and their products. For instance, the Lee Foundation for Nutritional Research of Milwaukee. This has as long ago as 1963 ascertained in a study that "pollen is so perfectly balanced a substance that one can live on it alone".

Happily enough, the prejudice against natural products is dwindling. The highly respected and well known Viennese professor, Karl Fellinger, for example, recently spoke of a positive attitude towards reliable natural medicaments on television.

Dependable help at menopause

Back to the practice of medicine.

Ideal "patient material" (an unseemly term, but one adopted in medicine) is available to Tekavčić, the head of a city clinic, in order to test the effectiveness of pollen. Women whose hormone systems had already "switched off", that is to say, who had entered menopause, came to him with clear climacteric symptoms.

On the other hand, there were women of the same age with menstruation who also suffered from climacteric symptoms, which doctors call pre-climacterium.

Those who have gone through it, know well of the complaints: sweating, sudden heat sensations (mainly in the face or in the head in general) also known as flushes, dizziness, sleeplessness, buzzing in the ears, fainting spells, paresthesia, pains in the heart region, breathlessness, increased blood pressure and mainly nocturnal aches and pains in the muscles, joints and bones as well as stomach and intestinal complaints, which can range from violent diarrhoea to stubborn constipation. None of this is a surprise. The female organism, used to discharging poisonous substances through menstruation for decades, has now not only to deal with the new hormonal situation, but also with the substances which previously were easily eliminated from the body, but which from this point on are dammed up in the body. (Alas, where are the old physicians who, in such circumstances mastered the procedures suitable in these cases, such as blood-letting, cupping glasses or leeches!)

Tekavčić decided to recheck the experiment. He divided 80 patients in the preclimacteric stage, (that is to say women who still menstruated but who had pronounced complaints) between 40 and 55 years old into two groups. The one group received a capsule of *Melbrosia p.l.d.* on an empty stomach each morning for two months, the second placebo without active substances.

For measuring purpose the body's weight is a good and simple guide.

Just about all women in this period of change gain "matron-meat" – additional weight. 29 of the Melbrosia group, which consisted in total of 38 women, lost weight during treatment, that means 52,6% lost weight – a significant result! Of the placebo group only four out of 36 women (11,1%).

The most important evaluation in the course of the investigation resulted from the so-called climacteric index (CI). The degree of severity of the climacteric symptoms was ascertained both before and after treatment by means of questioning. And Tekavčić himself was surprised; 35 of the 38 women treated with *Melbrosia p.l.d.* noted after the second month either the complete disappearance of the complaints or an extensive improvement, the percentage, 92,1! And the symptoms of 17 of this group before treatment had been really very, very bad. In comparison, the CI was reduced by only nine of 36 (25%) women in the control group.

Another investigation with eight patients in menopause (between 40 and 65 years old) finally convinced Tekavčić fully. The loss of weight was, for obvious reasons, indeed less spectacular than in the first test series ("only" 18 out of 37 women lost weight, that is 48%, whereas in the control group merely seven out of 38), but the climacteric index gave very positive results; 34 out of the 37 women treated with *Melbrosia p.l.d.* recorded either complete healing or very extensive and lasting improvement, that is once again 91,8%. (The control group: improvement in only ten out of 38 cases, that is 26,3%).

This treatment period, too, lasted for two months. You can take coals to Newcastle or take pollen to Sarajevo if it has to be expressly stated that the gynaecologist Osmanagić arrived at almost identical results! "The large majority (90%) of the ill women have demonstrated a more or less clearly recognizable good effect from this medicament".

Yet, another of pollen's facets is its very beneficial effect upon skin and connective tissue giving bestows women a considerably younger appearance than their years would suggest. The Australian television star, Hazel Phillips, who has been among the most avid of Melbrosia fans for years said: "The whole world thinks I take a rejuvenating pill! Thanks a lot . . .".

Little more has to be said about that.

CHAPTER 4

Cancer and radiation disease

Cancer, the fearsome scourge of the 20th century, is one mainly because official medicine commits its patients to three forms of therapy: surgical-steel, ray and chemotherapy.

Total cancer mortality remains, however, practically unchanged, as is verifyable in the official literature. In Austria, for example, stomach and intestinal cancer is receding, while lung cancer is on the increase [48].

There is no room for other forms of treatment in university medicine and what the professor of medicine rejects is not recognized by health insurance. Hence, each person who has survived one or more of the three official types of therapy for cancer patients and has been sent home either as "healthy" or "to die" (this happens, too!), has firstly to find the path to natural medicine himself, and secondly, to pay substantial sums for it. Nevertheless, newspapers and television, which have repeatedly attacked the problems of this inadequate therapy as well as that of subsequent-treatment have sometimes pioneered the formation of self-helping-groups. Where one victim informs and helps another.

This is not the place to thoroughly deal with natural medicine's treatment of cancer. This has already be done in an other place [56, p. 64 onwards]. The Viennese medical doctor, Dr. Richard Stöger, often recommends natural measures in his book [48] which is well worth reading.

Dr. Smolnig, a medical doctor from Carinthia (Austria) is, in fact, of the opinion the cancer is reversible* – a theory which orthodox doctors do not recognize [46]. I as a layman do not know, but do think that it is better, when suffering from cancer, to stay with a doctor who fights along with the patient (and *along with nature,* not against it) rather than give up. Not only Gerson [22] has impressively proved that cancer is essentially curable, but also many others (Breuss, Snegotska, Brauchle). It is not even so much a question of effort, which is very considerable in the case of Gerson's tumour-aggressive diet, but rather in on first place, one of diet and behaviour.

As with all illnesses of the system (cardiac and circulatory disorders, multiple sclerosis), the most broadly planned treatment possible is required. Correct, frugal nourishment at the right time of day is just as important as sufficient sleep, fresh air, a pleasant surrounding and supportive mental treatment [58, page 64 onwards].

Once again, I will mention the aspect of "fate".

There are cancer victims who are incurable cases in which even the almost superhuman skill of the great natural practitioners (Issels, Ardenne, Smolnig, Felbermayer) fails – such as the forty-year-old woman, one of my aquaintances, who for months has been wasting away because of inoperable breast-cancer and has responded to no treatment whatsoever – but that is rather an exception than the rule. Be careful, many doctors want to convince us that, as a rule, cancer is inescapable, because they do not know any better...!

One must, as a basic principal, search for alternatives and fight for one's life.

It would be presumptious to claim here that bee-

---

* This means that a cancer cell can return to being a healthy, no longer degenerated cell.

products are effective against cancer. They are not. Neither pollen, gelée royale nor propolis, kills cancer cells.

But the war against cancer is not only the killing of the enemy. This because pollen and gelée royale work regeneratively and propolis as a disinfectant and a consequently use against all types of micro-organisms, as was described in the previous chapter. Suppose we are confronted with a cancer victim, whose organism has been weakened and is badly in need of strengthening and is susceptible to infection; we cannot go wrong in supposing that such products can help this person.

And even quite considerably.

Russian investigations have shown that bee-keepers not only have an above-average life expectancy, but furthermore they hardly ever suffer from cancer. I am not quite able to believe that this is just coincidence.

Radiation disease eliminated

Cancer is an imminently pressing problem, and there are so many charlatans and miracle-healers in this field, that one does well to substantiate each and every statement. It will be proven here that pollen and gelée royale are not only capable of improving the cancer victims' general condition, but also that they can be a valuable support for official procedures, for example, for radiotherapy.

The snag is then once again, where is a radio-therapist to be found, who will leave natural medicine's methods untarnished in his clinic?

Sometimes coincidence helps – those, that is, who believe in it. Others call significantly related occurences without obvious causal relationship, synchronicity – and they are no less right than those who support coincidence [59]. Or was it just the power of observation, which caused Professor Osmanagić to notice that pollen and gelée royale have exhibited a positive effect on patients who had been operated for cancer and had undergone ray-treatment?

16 women castrated by operation or ray-treatment (or translated from medical terminology into straightforward colloquial English; women whose wombs had been removed or destroyed because of cancer and also their ovaries) received *Melbrosia p.l.d.* capsules from Osmanagić, in fact, two a day on an empty stomach half an hour before eating. The regenerative effect was fully noticeable after only ten days: "As a consequence of radiation disease the parenchymatous and blood-forming organs, the liver and the bone-marrow, are particularly damaged. It was at precisely this point, the effect was most clearly visible" (Osmanagić). The general condition improved to such an extent that almost all the women were able to return to their normal work, and that after severe radiation illness with sickness and bed-confinement.

When radiotherapy was continued the liver condition of ten of the 16 patients remained normal, although it had been very bad before the Melbrosia-treatment. The red blood cell formation of nine of the women improved as did the white blood cells of another nine [34].

These observations motivated other doctors to pursue the matter.

The Director of physical medicine, Dr. Franz Klemens Feiks, at the Klosterneuburg Hospital (near Vienna) was worried at the health of 17 patients, who could not eat any more, who vomited

30

continuously and who were tormented by terrible nausea as a result of powerful X-ray-treatment (250 roentgens per sitting and at least ten sittings). High doses of vitamins, anabolics and standard chemical treatments were ineffectual. Having been informed of Osmanagić's observations. Feiks gave each of the 17 women three capsules of *Melbrosia p.l.d.* a day for three weeks.

The symptoms of radiation disease disappeared completely in all 17 cases.

Then Feiks went one step further. 37 patients received Melbrosin *before* ray-treatment, when radiation illness occured in only a single case! Feiks noted in his publication, as being particularly interesting, that one woman had to interrupt the treatment for a week. Although she did not undergo radiotherapy, she got the feared X-ray hangover, because she had not taken the Melbrosin [16].

A control group consisted of 30 patients. They received ray-treatment without the pollen preparation. Here seven women became ill with radiation symptoms.

And an important side-effect: Loss of weight, so feared by cancer patients undergoing radiotherapy, was able to be held within reasonable limits. While each woman in the control group lost on an average 1,2 kilogrammes, those in the Melbrosia group lost just 0,3 kilogrammes.

Better sleep, normalized stool

The Indonesian doctors, Didid Tjindarbumi, Event Poetiray and Togar Simandjuntak of the surgical clinic at the University of Djakarta, have researched further, noteworthy, scientific work on cancer and pollen/gelée royale. They and the head of their clinic, Oetama, found Osmanagić's and Feiks' results to be interesting enough to check them out for the benefit of their own cancer patients. Using randomized methods they selected 60 cancer victims (52 women, eight men) in various stages of the illness. Some patients were in-operable, others had been operated on and had received ray-treatment. All of them received a Flora-poll capsule three times a day before eating. "The doomed", capsules only . . .

After eight months of observation, during which the doctors concerned themselves not only with blood and urine analysis, but also attached great importance to the evaluation of the appearance and the feelings of their patients, they established the following:

● No more weight was lost. After six weeks of Florapoll treatment each cancer victim had gained an average of 0,6 kilogrammes.
● 41 (70%) felt subjectively better and increased their activities. They had greater resistance and went for longer walks.
● 55 (90%) registered an increased appetite. This stayed with them until four weeks after treatment and then fell away again rapidly. The other ten percent of the patients, who continued without appetite were the most severly ill.
● Bowel function and movement (normalization, no diarrhoea or constipation resulting from radiotherapy) improved with 42 patients (70%). The remaining 18 announced no chance; they had not any problems with defecation previous to treatment.
● 60% of the patients announced better and

deeper sleep. This is especially important for cancer victims. It is the ones who sleep well, who lose the least or who even gain some who fare the best.

The doctors noted that malignant tumours were "apparently not directly affected" by Florapoll, and furthermore that "changes of the size of tumours are very difficult to determine". Only three patients complained of increased temperature in the cancerous ulcer's region, and this statement could not be confirmed by the doctors.

Were there side-effects? In the case of pollen and bee-preparations there is the opinion that allergies often occur . . . well.

In the pollen-specialists' practice for many years now, there have been hardly any pollen-allergies, not even in the cases of those who are notoriously allergic.

Feiks reported ten percent of the cases as having urticaria (nettle rash). The Indonesian doctors who observed their patients for eight months, did not find such a rash, but observed:

● two subjective cases of increased temperature
● three cases of disturbed sleep.

Consequent treatment with the pollen/gelée royale preparation led in each case to the end of the problems within ten days. A single patient, complaining of violent sweating, refused to continue the treatment [53].

If, finally, a conclusion can be drawn, then certainly it is that nothing is more essential for cancer victims than offering them a positive attitude towards their illness. To give assurance that

33

the body and soul arc not going down but rather up-hill. I believe that these bee-products have de-livered the proof that they can, in this area, con-siderably help the cancer victim.

And, contrary to X-ray-treatment and cytosta-tics (chemical medicaments which limit cell growth, and certainly not only that of cancerous cells, but that of the healthy ones, too) here the most ancient and important of medical principles is at work; Nil nocere. Damage nothing.

CHAPTER 5

There is no substitute for quality

There is no substitute for quality – this is above all a truth in the art of healing.

I have just said "art of healing" consciously. Talent is indispensable for medical practice, and, of course, good sound training, too. But the university professor, Dr. Gottfried Keller, the head of histology and embryology of the faculty of medicine at the University of Vienna, once said to me, "one is born to be a physician, but "physician" and "doctor of medicine" may not necessarily coincide". Before him, the Privy Councillor for medicine, Prof. Dr. Ernst Schweninger, who demonstrated the power of natural medicine on Bismarck (other doctors, with their orthodox methods had previously failed) stated: "I still believe that the best classification of doctors is among the artists . . . an artist is born, then he acquires his skills . . ." [45].

Not the titles nor the quantity of (the often repeated) publications demonstrate the ability of a doctor, neither does misunderstood scientific methodology nor his place within medicine's hierarchy. The critical matter is what he does for his patients.

In this field quantity precludes quality.

As one of Austria's most gifted, but hopelessly overworked surgeons (director, university professor, cancer specialist) said in answer to my question, whether or not he should treat at least one single patient exactly, polyvalently (with many methods) and with non orthodox procedures, "I have just come from sixty cancer cases . . .".

So then, one of my first suggestions to all who seek aid:

Out of the treadmill! Reflect! Think! Hardly anybody can become healthy in this system of *do ut des* (I give in order that you might give), in this vicious circle of having to give and take. And certainly nobody at all in the official health system with its social-insurance-number automation; social insurance doctors have just five minutes for each patient, otherwise it will not work.

If he has that much time.

You will see, quality is impossible in state medicine.

The total physician, he who has experience in natural medicine (he does not have to be a doctor at all, he might well be a non-medical practioner or a health advisor) views people differently, because each person is different.

In the previous chapters I have tried to show the curative effects pollen and gelée royale can have, optimally in the known combination of capsule-preparations. Here lies a considerable wealth of experience, observation, knowledge of nature, of cosmic relationships.

And humility. Recognition of fate. Knowledge that nothing is certainly actualizeable.

Millions of people in the whole world, valuing the freshness of youth, in their later years, too, buouyancy, productiveness and mental as well as bodily mobility, take some pollen/gelée royale preparation daily, many of them Melbrosia capsules.

Best is to let it melt under the tongue half an hour before the first meal.

It does not have to be Melbrosin either. Knowing only this, I have used it on myself and on dozens of my acquaintances, but there are, certainly, many other good preparations. You just have to be careful that the processed pollen-products are clean, but here, nature regulates itself: poisonous pollen poisons the bee too. In such cases, the bee-keeper has suffered the sad loss of a swarm, but he now knows that he must now avoid that swarm's pollen.

And *important:* Gelée royale is the most expensive bee-product, and so, many a producer economizes a little. But that is wrong. Less than 30 milligrammes of gelée royale a day is of no use, and in the previous chapter it was shown that, in severe cases, double or triple dosages must be given. Melbrosin is a company with more than a quarter of a century of experience and has assured itself a high degree of sincerity and international reputation through working together with scientific institutions. Furthermore, Melbrosin's experts are in possession of a special procedure to keep the easily digestible glée royale stable.

By the way, there are not only capsules. *Melbrosin-propolis* has been developed as a special resorative and stimulant not only for the elderly but also for children and adolescents (colds, stress of school), it is a honey-like substance of pear juice, wheat-germ, pollen, propolis and gelée royale.

In the matter of health central Europeans are slightly shy and slightly ashamed, so I am not able, here, to reveal the names of the many prominent people in show business, on and off stage, who keep themselves in condition with pollen preparations. But I have already mentioned Australian television star, Hazel Philips and the highly talented and unbelievably vigorous British authoress, Barbara Cartland, of more than 300 books, are happy to be named. In England, where so much is thought of sport and fair play, "doping" with pollen preparations is nothing unusual among the athletes – because it has nothing to do with harmful doping but rather with additional nutrition. Football and Rugby teams, marksmen, the boxer, Cassius Clay (alias Muhammed Ali), weight lifters, runners and ski-jumpers, all utilize the strengthening effect of blossom-dust and gelée royale.

"Beauty must come from within", this phrase was coined by the natural physician Maurice Mességué. He, who commands a cosmetic empire wants to say here: Face-lotions, make-up and skin-cream can help a woman a lot. But they are just an aid in a programme of complete beauty.

William Shenstone wrote "healthiness is beauty" in the year 1764 – and Mességué is of exactly the same opinion. Impeccable beauty, a pure complexion and firm skin will not be attained with impure blood, a badly functioning intestinal tract, chronic nicotine and alcohol poisoning or even worse, diseases affecting the entire organism.

May he, who condemns everything to the realm of fable because he considers it to be fancy, hear of one last attempt which refutes at least this objection. The owner of a stable with the approval of a veterinarian, let his horses have some pollen as additional nutrition before racing. Not only did the trainer state that the strength of the animals was increased, the nervousness lowered and concentration capacity improved, but also the veterinarian was especially pleased with the glossy coats and that "defective" spots on the skin had disappeared within a few days. A single drop of bitterness: A horse needs rather a large quantity of pollen, about 500 Austrian shillings (approximately 35 U.S. dollars) a month. That could be around ten percent of the "cost of maintainance", but a number of stable owners think it is be worthwhile and could reappear as prize-money . . .

CHAPTER 6
Propolis – top secret

Only a short time ago, propolis was a matter for a few initiated persons. Even nutritional chemists and professors of pharmacy considered its effects to be a figments of the imagination. And how should they have known otherwise, neither the Roman natural scientist, Pliny, nor the Greek physician, Dioscorides, was to be found in their reading matter.

Now one could reasonably believe that it would be better to replace propolis, a highly effective antibiotic, with modern pharmaceuticals.

First of all, it has not been replaced, because in order to replace something, it must have been previously known, and that cannot be asserted by the present pharmacists. And the "better" is not right at all.

Also to avoid natural medicine's boring lamentation about the dangers of antibiotics, the following should be said: The effectiveness of penicillin, streptomycin, chloramphenics and all other antibiotics (they are also natural substances) must

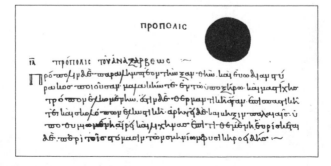

be honoured – many illnesses have been eliminated through them.

It is the reckless, wide spectrum employment of them that has caused world-wide resistent strains of bacteria and proliferating fungi to arise, which could become much more dangerous for mankind than the bacteria which would have been quite easily managed by other means. All of that would not have happened with propolis.

The Greek word Πρόπολις is "propolis – top secret".

It means simply "in front of the city", and, metaphorically, "the guards" – those which prevent things forcing their way into the community, thing which should stay outside.

And its use is already becoming clear. This substance prevents diseases from penetrating the hive. Infections have a devastating effect upon a swarm of bees – and these creatures themselves take precautions against such occurences.

It can no longer be established who coined the expression. It may well be supposed that Varro, Pliny and Dioscorides, the ancient authors, who gave the most thorough reports of bee-products, recorded that which had already been in use for a long time. Marcus Terentius Varro*: "They call that 'propolis' out of which they (the bees) make a protection in the hive's entrance in high summer.

It is used with the same name by doctors for poultices, for which reason it is more expensive than honey in the Via Sacra".

Varro also writes about the bee-bread (honeycomb pollen).

---

* Varro Reatinus" (116-27 b.C.), Rerum Rusticarum III, XVI, 23: Propolim vocant, e quo faciunt ad foramen introitus protectum ante alvum maxime aestate. Quam rem etiam nomine eodem medici utuntur in emplastris, propter quam rem etiam carius in sacra viam quam mel venit.

Even then it was considerably more precious and expensive than honey and was called 'Erithace'. Aristotle knew of it too. Although an all-rounder a philologist, politician and historian), Varro was surprisingly well informed about the behaviour of bees. For example, that they do not get honey, pollen, propolis and wax from the same plant.

Pliny even determines three resin-like substances, commosis, pissoceros and propolis, and all three are "of considerable medicinal use" [40]*.

Although no doctor, Pliny knew of propolis as a component of drawing ointments. He reported it eased pain and removed worked in thorns. Galen knew of utilizing propolis just as Alexander Trallianus and the gynaecologist, Moschion, and the famous Dioscorides wrote: "Propolis (is to be collected), the yellow and pleasant-smelling and (always) soft (substance) and is easily spread, like a mastic, even in a very dry condition. It is very warm and has drawing force; it draws out thorns and splinters. In the form of steam (smoke) it helps against coughs and, directly applied, it removes rashes. It is found in the mouth of bee-hives and it has a wax-like nature"**. We have printed a facsimile of this passage at the beginning of this chapter from a tenth-century byzantine manuscript (with the kind permission of the Austrian National Library, Vienna [12]).

It is strange that this tradition was later interrupted. Many of today's bee-keepers also appear not to be fully informed, otherwise they would not have to be called upon to produce our valuable propolis.

---

* Pliny, Nat. hist. 11,4
** Diosc. II, 84

However, something like a Propolis-International has been developed in recent years. Many people interested in apiarian medicine have busied themselves with the standardisation of the primary products which had tended to differ greatly. The centres are Rumania, Yugoslavia, the Soviet Union, Poland, Czechoslovakia, Austria, Denmark, Sweden and Switzerland.

Propolis contains (almost) everything

Bees line their hive or their hollow tree with propolis and seal off the crevices with it – hence it is sometimes called resin mastic or resin cerate.

The entrance is made narrower and weatherproof with propolis, and everything considered to be a foreign body is covered with it. That could be a corpse which is too large to remove, such as that of a snake or a mouse, for instance. These caracasses are so cleverly covered by the bees with propolis and with wax, that they are comparable to embalmed mummies, and therefore do not present the hive with any danger of infection.

It can also be gathered with a grid, which the beekeeper has placed in the hive as a "propolis trap" to obtain the purest product possible (free of parts of bees, wood and sand).

The bee collects propolis primarily from poplars, horse chestnuts, birches, elms, alders, beeches and conifers. Chemists have found out that the proportion of resins is from ten to 70%, of waxes 15 to 40%, of oils two to ten percent and of the insoluble components four to 25%. Soviet researches has isolated a host of chemically highly interesting compounds in this bee-resin: aminoacids (from the pollen component, usually around five percent), the vitamins B, E, H, and P, fatty acids (mainly myristin acid, cinnamon acid, cinnamon alcohol, vanillin, isovanillin, chrysin, coffee acid, sorbic acid, benzoic acid, quercetin and tracer elements such as zinc, glucoside, tannate, polysaccharide, enzymes and flavones).

Pollen, a world of its own? Propolis, even more so. Exaggerating, it could almost be said: There appears to be almost nothing which might not be contained in pollen.

The supposition, that it is the multiplicity and the apparently optimal substance-coordination which underlies propolis' healing power, cannot go wrong. There is many a spectacular case: Propolis has proven itself to be effective where the standard chemist's repertoire has failed.

Read more about it in the next chapter.

CHAPTER 7

From fever blister to tennis-elbow

It has already been said that bees use propolis as an antibiotic. But it still has not been proven beyond a doubt, in the strict scientific sense of the word, that propolis does, in fact, so function.

Happily, numerous researchers have undertaken this work. As early as 1948, it was established in Denmark that propolis limits the growth of tuberculosis bacilli. Later investigations demonstrated that propolis was effective against 24 of the 39 tested strains of bacteria and against 20 out of the 20 (!) tested fungi. Especially important: Propolis is effective against Salmonella typhi – a considerable irritant at the present time!

The Slovak researchers Čižmárik and Trupl tested propolis on 18 types of dermathophytes (more than 40 strains) and found the bee-resin to be effective in 0,1% to 2% concentrations (according to the type of fungi). In another work, they report the "especially high effect of propolis on gram positive bacteria, in particular, on 35 strains of Staphylococcus aureus, which originate from clinical material with various grades of resistance (up to multi-resistent)". The extract in a two-percent concentration functions is a dependable bactericide". On the other hand, the effect on gram negative bacteria is surprisingly varying" [50].

The Polish professor, Stanislaw Scheller, did research on Candida albicans, Canadida paracrusei and Candida pseudotropicale, microorganisms responsible for troublesome vaginal inflammation.

Propolis had an excellent effect here [44]. The substance is administered in the form of vaginal suppositories. "The therapeutic effect occurs in 14 days, no relapse is observed" (Scheller).

Only a dermatologist can really appreciate the significance of these discoveries. Skin infections with pyogenic organisms are a big problem, just as dermatophytes (whether athlete's foot ringworm or vaginal fungi) and resistent bacteria are too. What a help propolis can be!

Stop – aren't we curing one evil with an even worse evil? Isn't this propolis maybe even worse? Doesn't it, perhaps, have an even more devastating effect upon the important intestinal flora (composed of "good" bacteria) than the other antibiotics?

There is no danger. Doctors have known this for more than 2000 years, and their knowledge has been completely confirmed in present times. There is no habituation to propolis in the sense that resistent strains of bacteria are cultivated in the body. There are no side-effects – except that around one percent of the patients develope allergies, especially against the pollen contained in resin. In this case treatment must be immediately stopped, then all complaints cease. Other than this single exception, no side-effects are known. Medicine also utilizises propolis for the regulation of intestinal function . . .

Propolis is probably even effective in one area where there had been, until now, little relief. As Osmanagić was able to demonstrate in extended observations at the University of Sarajevo, propolis in honey has a preventive effect on flu and colds.

63 out of 220 students volunteered to test pre-

ventives. That was in 1976, during the large Hong-kong-flu epidemic, with which as much as two thirds of the population became ill in some areas. After the epidemic, the results. Only six (nine per-cent) of the propolis consumers became ill, half of these, moreover, just three days after starting treat-ment ("too short a time to allow the propolis to attain its favourable effect" wrote Osmanagić), so infection may already have been at hand. Of the 157 students in the control group 61 (38,8%) be-came ill. This allows the conclusion that propolis is effective against viruses, perhaps even against virus particles. Also virus particles can still be pathogen.

A particularly unpleasant type are the Herpes viruses. Among other things, they cause Herpes zoster (shingles), Herpes genitalis, and Herpes labialis (aphthitis stomatosa), the bothersome blister rash on the mouth's mucous membrane, lips and in the region of the mouth, for which, until now, there was no remedy. Correctly said, co-cause, because, here also, the approach of total medicine differs fundamentally from official medicine's one-way chemotherapy. This takes some chemical substance or other and tries to poison the pathogenic agent, yet, the total physician knows that the agent must find suitable ground in order to thrive, and thus he attempts to made the environment healthy, that is, incom-patible for the agent.

Herpes-maladies are certainly not life-threat-ening but are painful, and itch. In order to stabilize the personal environment, a low-protein diet is essential (consult a doctor about natural-medicinal methods!), but as far as the agent is concerned, you can help yourself.

With propolis.

On the one hand, the attacked skin-area can be swabbed with an alcohol solution ("Propolis-Elixir"), on the other, propolis can be applied in the form of an ointment ("Salvacol", "Melbrosin", "Lebensbaum", "Tree of Life"). The pain-soothing effect occurs almost immediately; the complete cure takes some time, of course.

The bothersome acne

Propolis cream helps poorly healing wounds, ulcers, and nerve complaints (e.g. the nerves are involved with shingles), as Pliny already knew. In Russian clinics highly effective burn ointments contain propolis.

This complex bee product is of use not only with severe burns, but with yet another common skin problem, acne.

It is not only women in adolescence who are concerned here. A report from Vienna is about a 45-year-old woman, who had been suffering from a severe type-acne, conglobata, on her chin since she was 15 years old, that is for 30 years. Dozens of dermatologists and clinics had tried to heal her with the complete armoury of modern medicine. They had not economized on either antibiotics or cortisone. The first to try it with propolis was Dr. Edith Lauda of Vienna, and "after two treatments, the infiltrated skin regions were free of infection" (Lauda).

After a few weeks the acne was completely cleared up.

Thereupon, 59 more patients, some of whom had been suffering from acne for decades, received similar treatment. No fewer than 57 were healed with propolis ointment and propolis tincture!

One other case deserves mention. It demonstrates better than others the propolis effect on nerves, which the doctors of antiquity knew and valued.

The test case of sciatica

The Swede, Bertil Westerlund, suffered spinal-column injury when he was 13 years old. A year later he had severe pains. They would get better, then always reappear. When he was 46 and neither doctor nor hospital had been able to help him, he was sent into early retirement.

That is the typical reaction of the social state. This system is not prepared for a case of sciatica which resists all treatment for 33 years. Something had to happen (according to classic Viennese medical officialdom, "ut aliquid fit" – "in order that something happens"). So he was sent into retirement.

Thus was the conscience of the officials pacified, but Westerlund's pain was not eliminated.

One day, he could not get out of bed anymore. His wife had to lift him up, support him and dress him. The walk to the tobacconist's 25 yards away from his front door needed 20 minutes.

Bertil Westerlund was a severly disabled man.

Happily, a friend had heard of the new propolis ointment from Austria. He persuaded Bertil to try it, and it saved the Swede. Three days of treatment, three days of ointment compresses, and Bertil was able to walk upright again. A few days later, the pain was gone. For ever.

As far as that can be said now, two years later. Anyway, it has been gone until now.

By the way, ointment compresses: It has been mentioned above that the ancient physicians especially valued them. They already knew why.

One of the best examples, for their effectiveness is another application, which official medicine either does not know anything about, or recommends operation for: tennis-elbow. This is a very painful inflammation of the muscles, tendons or tendon sheaths (or of all of them) in the elbow region. Not only tennis players suffer from it, but also many others whose forearms are heavily taxed: typists, housewives, photographers. Here there has been spectacular success with propolis cream. The cream needs to be thickly applied three times a day; in stubborn cases, a compress (changed twice a day) is essential. After an initial increase of pain, a remarkable improvement occurs usually on the third day. After a week the pain usually disappears completely.

Important: immobile the arm; do not make many movements with the affected tendons. Once freed from pain, be careful for as long as possible.

In more than 80% of even the most stubborn cases, propolis cream produced a most successful result.

Comparable help can be expected for inflamed tendons in other parts of the body and also for bursitis.

CHAPTER 8

The stomach ulcer which disappeared

Propolis has a place in internal medicine, too. Director Feiks, from Klosterneuburg, who has already been spoken about concerning pollen, has been interested in pollen for a long time. The ancient physicians had treated intestinal ulcers with it – why should that nor be possible in the twentieth century?

In the Klosterneuburg Hospital the director observed 294 patients being treated there for ulcus venticuli or ulcus duodeni (gastric or duodenal ulcers). To one group of 108 patients, he gave five drops of propolis tincture to be drunk 15 minutes before each meal, in addition to the usual treatment. The control group, of 186 patients, received the normal treatment, however, without propolis.

Clinical termination of the problem occured in

	propolis patients	control group patients
less than 3 days	70%	10%
3 to 7 days	17%	15%
7 to 14 days	5%	30%
more than 14 days	3%	25%
no such termination	5%	20%
subsequent operation necessary	5%	15%

Not only was the healing more rapid but longer lasting – that was the spectacular result of this extended test-series. Feiks sums up: "It was not just that more than 90% of the propolis patients, as opposed to 55% of the control group, had no more complaints, but additionally that the number of operations during the stay in hospital was reduced to a third" [17].

An effect which is primarily of interest to the patients, but without doubt to the hospital management and social insurance as well. It would be a way of reducing the number and duration of absences through sickness even of reducing the number of operations. It must be said that no one on the side of the health authorities has yet been interested this result.

Hippocrates knew that "the best of two doctors is the one, who arrives at his goal with the means which are less drastic, and more gentle". Feiks treated 15 out-patients with ulcers (not in the above mentioned exstended test series) exclusively with propolis tincture – nothing else! Result: 14 regained health. Only one had to be sent to hospital later.

Feiks: "An 81-year-old patient came to me for treatment. Since she was 69 years old, she had had a callous ulcus ventriculi (stomach ulcer, the author). For cardiac reasons, she was not operated on. The X-ray check up each year had shown the ulcer to have remained unchanged. After six weeks of out-patient treatment, with the described method with propolis tincture only, the ulcer was classified radiologically as healed. It did not subsequently appear, and after the patient had died at age of 85, of an apoplectic stroke, there was no scar to be seen at the autopsy".

Troubles with spine

Director Dr. Emil Eckl at the Reutte Hospital in the Tyrol recorded the recent success of propolis in yet another test – a double-blind test.

And in a very important field; in that of HWS and BWS syndromes, in cases of muscle aches, lumbago and arthritis. (For those, who have happily never suffered from these: By HWS and BWS syndromes is meant various complaints, including stubborn headaches subdued by nothing, caused by irregularities in the regions of the neck, chest and spine. It ranges from the "whip-lash effect" of a car accident so spondylathrosis, from simple muscle and tendon tension to many-years-old discopathy ["slipped disk"])

28 patients received propolis ointment, a second group (also 28 people) received an ointment without effect substances, a placebo. The doctors did not know which ointment they were using. And here are the results:

	ointment 41	ointment 42
impressive improvement after 2 to 7 days of treatment	14	5
moderate improvement after 1 to 5 days	10	14
no improvement	4	9

The effective propolis ointment, as is easily recognizeable, must have been no. 41, ointment 42 was the placebo. Eckl: "In the double-blind test the superiority of ointment 41 was to be clearly noted in the cases of impressive improvement (14:5) and in the cases treated with no success (4:9) . . . Our previous experience with Melbrosin-Massage cream was thus verified: quicker and clearer relief of pain, decrease of morning-stiffness in cases of periphal joint-problems, good compatibility" [13].

Numerous doctors report the same success with this massage cream.

For instance, Dr. Werner Kleine of Munich, who had treated many patients having painful hip and knee joints for years that is, there were symptoms of wear and degeneration, as well as acute arthritis cases). In most cases, he has managed to relieve the pain within a week. In cases where complete healing has not been attained (16%), the pain receded significantly.

The company doctor of a large Viennese car firm, whose workers similarly suffer from forms of chronic arthritis (particularly gonarthritis, that is inflammation of the knee joint), has been using propolis ointment for years with good results.

And talking about legs, Russian pediatrists have been "pulling" corns with it for decades, just as general practitioners of many lands have been treating acute and chronic varicose veins with it (simply spread it lightly, do not massage), and dermatologists have been using it against in-grown and "fungi-eaten" toe-nails.

Or, if you as a man or woman of mature age suffer from cramps-angio-spasms caused by peripheral circulation disorder, which tends to appear in the legs in the evening, then you can take care of yourself very well with Melbrosin- (or Salvacol-) Massagecream. Here you must firmly massage it in – as opposed to varicose veins!

And it is best to do this every evening before going to bed because propolis has then time to work.

Propolis for oral inflammations

On the other end of the body propolis is useful, too. We have reported about the painful Aphthae (fever blisters), but it helps just about everywhere. In the eyes: conjunctivitis (two drops of Propolis-Elixir in an eye-bath with luke-warm water, rinse a few times every day). For styes, spread on propolis ointment lightly a few times every day.

In the ears: Infections of the inner and middle ear do not respond so well, however with abscesses in the outer auditory canal the remedy has proven its worth. ENT doctors, who, in opposition to original prejudices have tried it out, are amazed by the healing effect of the cream after small surgical operations upon the ear.

In the nose, throat and neck regions propolis also releases its disinfectant and healing power; all types of open areas, gingivitis, toothache, dental cavities, bad breath (foetor ex ore), nasal odour (ozaena) and many other complaints respond well to propolis.

The bothersome malady of civilization (or of degeneration?), paradontosis, the receding of the gums, cannot yet be healed with propolis, nonetheless most cases can be improved with it. Propolis-Gel has been developed especially for it; it contains the bee-healing principal in a water-soluble base – because it is not everyones cup of tea to chew raw propolis or to rub an oily ointment into the gums. The gel is simply spread onto the gums with a finger, and massaged in with slight pressure.

For combating throat-illnesses (tonsillitis, laryngitis) gargling is recommended; a couple of drops of propolis solution in a glass of luke-warm water. Or even easier, propolis lozenges can be taken when necessary. They are sucked and dissolve, the resulting propolis-saliva moistens the tonsils and larynx – an application which is friendly to the body and also optimally effective. It is recommended after tonsils-operations; it accelerates the healing!

The dentist has to look after toothache, but you can prevent most cavities with a newly developed propolis toothpaste. The pain-soothing and anti-biotic qualities of propolis can often help in cases of sudden toothache – when a dentist is not around. You rub the gums around the painful tooth with Propolis-Elixir of Propolis-Gel and massage a bit of ointment – into the neck!

The difficult Psoriasis

Propolis for skin-diseases – most of this has already be spoken about. There are also lotions with propolis (Salvaskin Facial Lotion, Melbrosin-Facial Lotion) which help in light acne and with impure skin and sebum problems (Seborrhoea). Psoriasis, which is unfortunately wide-spread, responds well to treatment with propolis ointment. It is important that the patient stays with a strict diet (no alcohol, no nicotine, little protein, and when so, only the highest of quality), in this manner, the internal measures are complete. Psoriasis is often coupled with arthritic, rheumatic and liver complaints. Since it has been proven that propolis (pollen and gelée royale have a positive effect upon blood, the liver and the RES (reticulo-endo-thelial system) which is very important for remaining healthy, the taking of drops is advisable as follows: five drops in a half a glass of water three times a day, best before meals. Of course, the combi-preparation Melbrosin-Propolis can also be taken.

By the way; hepatitis (including serum hepatitis A and B), jaundice and other liver complaints can be treated with propolis with confidence. The doctor will find his work much easier!

Propolis heals haemorrhoids

The Hepatic-Portal vein; a problem area for many who follow sitting professions. No one speaks with pleasure about haemorrhoids, and no one at all wants to have them.

Propolis is good here, too.

In the Alps, but also in Russia, in France and in the forests of the North the tradition has remained of preparing haemorrhoid-ointments out of the resin of many trees. Spruce, fir, larch, birch. Such resin-ointments are often a dependable aid when the pain is unbearable. Propolis ointment works the same way, but better. It should also be, when necessary, inserted. In addition it should be born in mind that the intestines love damp surroundings; washing directly after bowel movement is almost as good. Flatulent foods and alcohol are to be avoided.

The kidneys, the bladder, the prostate gland can equally profit from propolis. In the first days of trouble (inflammation, colds, irritation) larger doses; ten drops of elixir three times a day or ten lozenges. After three days reduce to a third, but continue the treatment for ten days.

The same for constipation. Propolis-lactose capsules (milk-sugar as base) have been developed. Often elderly people suffer from constipation – and just how useful a gentle but highly effective bowel regulant can be for the severely ill has been shown in chapter 3. This preparation has proven its worth not only in cases of stubborn constipation but also of diarrhoea and any irregular bowel activity, typical in cases of intestinal damage by antibiotics and radiation damage. One capsule three times a day – for two weeks! After that you are rid of annoyance and can stop, or you continue with reduced doses.

You can keep on taking three capsules a day without hesitation. That will certainly not damage your health.

And since we are still in this area; the chafing which occurs between the thighs after long waltes with some sweating, can be eliminated inside two days with Melbrosin-Massage cream or Salvacol-Massage cream.

Some natural physicians would like to believe that they have observed propolis effect against the loss of hair. That should not be challenged, but also not confirmed; I do not know of a single case. But then it has tonic effect on elderly citizens, especially in the form of the Melbrosin-Propolis preparation, which additionally strengthens the heart and shows a water-reducing effect on dropsy of the heart. Sleeplessness, nervousness, fatigue, general tiredness – this preparation is just right for these! Furthermore it regulates blood-pressure, which is desired, especially in geriatrics. It does not cure arteriosclerosis, but it does have a broad prophylactic effect. A newly developed propolis shampoo makes the hair shine, the dandruff disappear and leaves the skin with good circulation. For all people with hair problems.

Women's illnesses

Investigations relevant here have already been cited. But it can be said in summary; propolis was known in antiquity for its regulating and soothing effect on menstruation.

Dysmenorrhoea and amenorrhoea can be combated with either propolis tincture (five drops twice a day) or lozenges. Ovary and fallopian tube inflammation can be treated internally (drops) and externally (ointment). For vaginitis, leucorrhoea, trichonomasis and similar bacterial and fungal infections of the vagina, propolis vaginal suppositories can be used. Where not available. Tincture-saturated tampons can be inserted.

* * *

This should be an abridged survey of the large area of apiarian medicine. I hope I have not forgotten anything essential, regardless of the presentation's concise form.

Although I have been investigating and engaging the intuition and imagination of people interested in natural medicine, the many forms of medication which I have tried to describe to you can certainly be multiplied . . .

Literature

1. Alexander Trallianus seu Alexander Yater: Werke. Brau-müller, Wien 1878–1879.
2. Aschner, Bernhard: Lehrbuch der Konstitutionstherapie. Hippokrates, Stuttgart 1933.
3. Atyasov, N. I., Guseva, M. P., und Kupriyanov, V. A.: Die Behandlung granulierender Wunden mit Propolis-Salben. UdSSR, o. J.
4. Bachmann, Christian: Die Krebsmafia. Tomek, Monaco 1981.
5. Binder, Walter: Kittharz – die antibiotische Alternative. Naturheilpraxis 5/79.
6. Brauchle, Alfred: Das große Buch der Naturheilkunde. Prisma, Gütersloh 1977.
7. Brondegaard, V. J.: „Harz" als Heilmittel in der Volksme-dizin. Österreichische Apotheker-Zeitung, 33. Jg., 51/52 (22. 12. 1979).
8. Breuß, Rudolf: Ratschläge zur Vorbeugung und Behand-lung vieler Krankheiten. Krebs, Leukämie und andere scheinbar unheilbare Krankheiten mit natürlichen Mitteln heilbar. Eigenverlag, Bludenz o. J.
9. Čižmárik, J., und Trupl, J.: Propolis-Wirkung auf Hautpil-ze. Pharmazie, 31 (1976).
10. –, –: Wirkung von Propolis auf Bakterien. Ebenda.
11. Dethlefsen, Thorwald: Schicksal als Chance. Bertelsmann, Gütersloh 1980.
12. Dioskorides, Pedanios: Materia medica. Paris 1935.
13. Eckl, Emil: Erfahrungen mit Melbrosin-(Salvacol-)Mas-sage-Creme in der Behandlung schmerzhaft-entzündlicher Prozesse im Doppelblindversuch. Reutte 1980.
14. Evers, Joseph: Warum Evers-Diät? Haug, Heidelberg 1974.
15. Feiks, Franz Klemens: Application locale d'extrait de propolis dans le traitement du zona. In 54.
16. –: The effect of florapoll on the irradiation syndrome and in the climacterium virile. Klosterneuburg 1974.
17. –: Über eine neue Möglichkeit der konservativen Thera-phie der Ulcuskrankheit.
18. Filipič, B. et Likar, M.: Activité antiherpétique de la propolis, de la gelée royale et de l'interferon. In 54.

19. –, –: Inhibitory effect of propolis an royal jelly on some viruses. Interferon Scientific Memoranda, Buffalo, USA., April 1976.
20. Funke, Hans: Das Phänomen der Phytonzide. Naturheilpraxis 2/80.
21. Galenos, Klaudios: Opera omnia. Hervagius et Frobenius, Basileae 1538.
22. Gerson, Max: Eine Krebs-Therapie. 50 geheilte Fälle. Hyperion, Freiburg 1961.
23. Hanssen, Maurice: The healing power of pollen. Thorsons, Wellingborough 1979.
24. Hill, Ray: Propolis, the natural antibiotic. Thorsons, Wellingborough 1977.
25. Karimova, Z. Kh., und Rodionova, E. N.: Die Verwendung von Propolis in der Behandlung der Lungen- und Bronchientuberkulose. UdSSR, o. J.
26. Kern, Maks: Propolis als Heilmittel in der otorhinolaryngologischen Praxis. Ljubljana, o. J.
27. Kern, Maks., Šobu, Erika et Budihna, Marjan· Apicomplex comme produit protecteur dans le cas du radiummucositis. In 54.
28. Kivalkina, V. P., Belozerova, G. A., et Kamalov, G. H.: La stimulation de l'immunogenèse avec propolis dans l'immunisation des animaux à la maladie Aueski. In 54.
29. Mavrić, N., Osmanagić, I. et Volić, E.: Le traitement des dystrophies du col uterin par la propolis. In 54.
30. Mességué, Maurice: Heilkräuterlexikon Molden, Wien 1976.
31. –: Von Menschen und Pflanzen. Molden, Wien 1972.
32. Moschionos: Peri ton gynaikeion pathon. Gräffer et Soc., Wien 1793.
33. Orkin, V. F.: La propolis dans le traitement de la prostatite chronique. In 54.
34. Osmanagić, Izet: A clinical testing of the effect of the preparation „florapoll" in cases of the irradiation syndrome carried out at the Endocrinological Departement of the University Clinic for women of the Medical Faculty in Sarajevo. Sarajevo, 1973.
35. –: Doppelblindtest mit Melbrosia executive bei verminderter Beischlaf- und Zeugungsfähigkeit der Männer. Sarajevo 1979.
36. –: Klinische Überprüfungen der Wirkung des Präparates Melbrosia p.l.d. bei Frauen mit klimakterischen Syndrom

an der endokrinologischen Abteilung der Universitäts-
frauenklinik der medizinischen Fakultät in Sarajevo. Sarajevo, 1972.

37. –: Report of the preventive properties of propolis against
influenza. Sarajevo 1976.

38. Osmanagić, I., Biljenki, D., Mavrić, N.: L'action thérapeu-
tique des „Melbrosia" dans la maladie d'irradiation. In 54.

39. Osmanagić, I., Mujezinović, N., Pokrajčić, Lj.: Le traitement de la dysménorrhée avec melbrosin chez les adoles-
centes. In 54.

40. Plinius, Gaius Secundus: Naturae historiarium libri
XXXVII. Gothae 1855.

41. Popesković, D., Khanfar, M. H., Petrović, Z., et Dimitrije-
vić, M.: L' etude parallele de l'action des fractions de
propolis sur les cultures trichomonas (T. vaginalis, T.
gallinae et T. microti). In 54.

42. Reuben, David: Diät, die das Leben rettet vor Krebs,
Infarkt. Desch, München 1976.

43. Rooks, V. P.: The use of propolis in the treatment of
non-specific endobronchitis. UdSSR, o. J.

44. Scheller, Stanislaw: In-vitro-Untersuchungen der Emp-
findlichkeit von Candida auf Propolis. Initiale Beurteilung
von Propolispräparaten in der Behandlung der von Candida verursachten Vaginaentzündungen. Polen 1980.

45. Schweninger, Ernst: Der Arzt. Madaus, Radeburg 1926.

46. Smolnig, Erich: Die Demaskierung des Krebsproblems.
Carinthia, Klagenfurt 1979.

47. Snegotska, Otto: Krebs, Diagnose und Therapie. Eigenverlag, Berlin 1976.

48. Stöger, Richard: Älter werden – aber ohne Krebs. Mau-
drich, Wien 1981.

49. Suchy, Henryk: Bestimmung der Sensitivität von Trichomonas vaginalis auf Propolis. Goczalkowice Zdroj (Polen)
1978.

50. Suchy, Henryk, et Suchy, Maria: L' action de la propolis et
du produit melbrosia chez les femmes avec le syndrome
ménopausique. In 54.

51. Tanasienko, Y. S.: The use of propolis for the prophylaxis
and treatment of chronic and non-specific inflammation of
the lungs and bronchial-asthma of children. UdSSR, o. J.

52. Tekavčić, Bogdan: Clinical examinations on dysmenorr-
hoe in girls and the climacteric syndrome in women.
Ljubljana, o. J.

53. Tjindarbumi, Didid; Poetiray, Evert, and Simandjuntak, Togar: The use of florapoll as supplement therapy to various malignant cancer cases in the departement of surgery, Dr. Tjipto Margunkusumo Hospital. Jakarta 1974.
54. Troisième Symposium International d'Apitherapie. September 1978, Portorož, Yougoslavie.
55. Tsitsin, N.: Studies on elder people. Moscou, o. J.
56. Uccusic, Paul: Naturheiler. Ariston, Genf 1978.
57. –: Nur die Natur heilt. In: Imago mundi 1980.
58. –: PSI-Resümee. Ariston, Genf 1975.
59. Urban, Peter: Parapsychologie – Schicksalsforschung zwischen Psychologie und Astrologie. Herder, Wien 1974.
60. Varro, Marcus Terentius: Rerum rusticarum libri tres ex recensione Henrici Keil. Lipsiae 1884.
61. Vasilev, V., Manova-Kanazireva, St., und Todorov, V.: Heilung von Moniliasis albicans und Intertrigo bei Säuglingen mit Propolis. Sofia, o. J.

Index

Medical terms in bold-face type. Short references to treatment. The numbers refer to the page numbers.

---

* Different according to the country. Available in Austria as "Diaformin".

Cancer: 27 onwards

Catarrh: Propolis lozenges, Melbrosin-Propolis 37

Chafing: (inflamed skin between the legs; intertrigo), Salvacol-Cream a few times each day 58

Circulation: 20

Colds: Melbrosin-Propolis for prevention. Internal: propolis lozenges. For the nose, Tampons saturated with Melbrosia-propolis elixir 46

Colitis: Propolis-lactose capsules 57

Complexion: Salvaskin-Gesichtswasser (face-lotion) 38-39

Conjunctivitis: see eye infection

Constipation: up to three propolis-lactose capsules a day 32, 57

Contusions: Salvacol-Cream 49-50

Corns: Salvacol-Creme 54

Cosmetics: Melbrosin-Gesichtswasser (face lotion) 38

Cough: Propolis lozenges 42

Cuts: see injuries

Cystitis: five drops of melbrosia-propolis elixir in half a glass of water before meals. In acute cases, up to five times each day. Between meals suck propolis lozenges 37

Dandruff: Propolis shampoo 58

Deficiency diseases: Melbrosia capsules, Melbrosin-Propolis, Florapoll 20-21

Dermatosis: Salvacol-Cream 42, 56

Diarrhoea: Propolis-lactose capsules 32, 46

Disinfection: see antiseptic

Dislocations: Salvacol-Cream 49-50

Dropsy of the heart: Melbrosin-Propolis, one tea-spoon three times a day 37, 58

Ear trouble: 24, 55

Eczema: Melbrosin-Gesichtswasser (face lotion), Salvacol-Cream. Internal: Melbrosin-Propolis and Florapoll. Diet!

Effusions: rub lightly with Salvacol-Cream

Enterocolitis: as intestinal infection

Eye infection: fill eye-bathing glass (or cupped hand) with luke-warm water plus three drops of melbrosia-propolis elixir, bath eye. If necessary, a few times each day 55

Face care: Salvaskin-, Melbroskin-Gesichtswasser (face lotion) 47

Fever: Propolis lozenges, Melbrosia capsules 47

Flatulence: Propolis-lactose capsules up to three a day. Take care of your diet 57

Flu: Melbrosin-Propolis 47

Frigidity: Melbrosia p.l.d. 19 onward

Furunculosis: External: Melbrosia-propolis elixir and Salvacol-Cream. Internal: Melbrosia capsules and Melbrosin-Propolis. Diet!

Gastritis: see intestinal infection

Gastroenteritis: as intestinal infection

Geriatrics: Melbrosia Executive, Melbrosia p.l.d., Melbrosin-Propolis 14, 36

Glands, swollen: along side medical treatment, rub in Salvacol

Gums, bleeding: Propolis-Gel, propolis toothpaste 55

Gums, damaged: massage in Propolis-Gel 55

Haemarrhoids: Salvacol-Cream 57 onward

Halitosis: (Foetor ex ore), propolis lozenges, rinse mouth out with diluted Melbrosia-propolis elixir; if necessary intestinal stabilization with propolis-lactose 57

Headaches: 20

Heart, stimulation and support: along side conservative medical treatment, Melbrosia Executive, Melbrosia p.l.d. 19, 24, 37, 58

Hepatitis: 57

Herpes virus: Melbrosia-propolis elixir 47 onward

Hormonal system: 16,x1

Impotence: Melbroisa Executive 16

Indigestion: Propolis-lactose capsules, Florapoll 59

Infection: propolis in every form 29, 46

Injuries: Melbrosia-propolis elixir undiluted (builds protective film and disinfects), for quicker healing and better cicatrising Salvacol-Cream 48

Insect bites: Salvacol-Cream

Intertrigo: Salvacol-Creme a few times a day (for adults as well as for infants) 60

Intestinal damage due to antibiotics: diet; a lot of yoghurt. Kephir and Propolis-lactose capsules for support 41, 46, 57

Intestinal infection: five drops of Melbrosia-propolis elixir in half a glass of water half an hour before each meal 12, 46, 51 onward

Intestinal inflammation: see intestinal infection

Itching: Salvacol-Cream. Swab with Melbrosia-propolis elixir 48

Kidney trouble: as cystitis

Laxative: Propolis-lactose capsules 32, 57

Leg, open sores: rub in Salvacol-Cream lightly a few times each day

Leucorrhoea: see vaginitis

Limitation of infection: with all propolis preparations

Liver: Melbrosin-Propolis 19, 30, 56

Liver, decontamination of: Florapoll, Melbrosia Executive 30

Loss of weight: Melbrosia p.l.d. 25

Menopause: Melbrosia p.l.d. 20 onward, 23 onward

Menstruation: control, painful, too strong, too weak, Melbrosia p.l.d. 19 onward, 22

Metabolism, stimulation of: Propolis-lactose, Melbrosin-Propolis, Florapoll 57-58

Migraines: 20

Moniliasis albicans: (Bacterial infection of the oral cavity of newly born!), tampon affected area, tampons saturated with Melbrosin-propolis elixir, alcohol, honey, water 55

Mucous membranes, enflamed and swollen: spread Propolis-Gel softly or rinse with luke-warm water with five drops of Melbrosia-propolis elixir 55

Muscle aches, spained muscles: massage with Salvacol-Cream 24, 53 onward

Nail-bed suppuration: Melbrosia-propolis elixir (swab with undiluted), Salvacol Cream

Nasal infection, odour from the nose: insert tampons saturated with Melbrosia-propolis elixir 55

Neck pains: massage firmly with Salvacol-Creme 53 onward

Nerves, pain and alleviation: spread Salvacol-Cream lightly 48 onward

Nettle rash: Salvacol-Cream: if allergy to pollen or propolis suspected, stop taking preparation 33

Neuralgia: rub in Salvacol lightly 48 onward

Onychitis: see nail-bed suppuration

Oral infection: rinse with five drops of Melbrosia-propolis elixir in a glass of water a few times a day. Spread Propolis Gel onto painful spots. 55

Overweight: 25

Paradontosis: massage the gums with Propolis-Gel (a few times a day), suck propolis lozenges, rinse with Melbrosia propolis elixir

Pharyngitis: as angina tonsillaris

Phlebitis: along side normal medical measures, spread Salvacol-Cream lightly. Internal: propolis lozenges or Melbrosin-Propolis 19

Pleurisy: along side medical measures; External: Salvacol-Cream for soothing pain. Internal: Melbrosia-propolis elixir in water and propolis lozenges to combat infection

Portal vein: infection of 57

Postrate gland: (infection, enlargement), Propolis suppositories or rectally Salvacol-Cream, also massage cream externally. Internal: treatment as with cystitis, additionally Melbrosia Executive 19

Psoriasis: Salvacol-Cream; diet and plenty of sun! 56

Pyelitis: as cystitis

Radiation disease: 27 onward, 58

Resistance, strengthening of the body's: Melbrosia p.l.d., Melbrosia Executive, honey, Melbrosin-Propolis 29

Rheumatism: Internal: Melbrosin-Propolis; External: massage Salvacol-Cream firmly into painful areas 56

Scalds: Melbrosia-propolis elixir (builds protective film), Salvacol-Cream 48

Sciatica: massage in Salvacol-Cream a few times a day 49, 53

Seborrhoea: Salvaskin, Melbroskin 56

Sensitivity to weather changes: Melbrosin-Propolis

Shingles: swab with undiluted Melbrosia-propolis elixir 47-48

Shoulder-arm syndrome: massage with Salvacol-Cream 53

Skin-disease: see respective heading. Basically Melbrosia-propolis elixir (concentrated or diluted) or Salvacol-Cream 26, 42, 45, 54

Skin eruption, herpetic: Salvacol-Creme 45

Skin, oily and impure: Salvaskin-Gesichtswasser (face lotion) 46, 55

Sores, festering: Melbrosia-propolis elixir: Salvaskin-Gesichtswasser (face lotion) (for pustules), Melbroskin-Gesichtswasser (face lotion) 46, 55

Sport medicine: External (strained, sprained, pulled muscles and tendons): Salvacol-Cream; Internal (generative): Florapoll and Melbrosia capsules 38

Sprains: Salvacol-Cream 49-50

Sterility: 16 onward

Stimulant: Melbrosin-Propolis, Melbrosia capsules 16, 29, 58

Stimulation of the brain: Melbrosia Executive, Melbrosia p.l.d. 20

Strengthening: Melbrosia Executive (for men), Melbrosia p.l.d. (for women), in general and for children Melbrosin-Propolis 16 onward, 36, 58

Stress: Melbrosia Executive 19, 37

Sunburn: Salvacol-Cream

TB: 45

Tennis-elbow: rub in Salvacol at least three times a day. In stubborn cases an ointment compress for some days 12, 50

Throat, sore: as angina tonsillaris

Toothache: massage Propolis-Gel into the gums around the painful tooth; rinse with Melbrosin-propolis elixir 55

Tuberculosis: pulmonary 45

Tumor: 29 onward

Ulcerative stomatitis: see halitosis

Ulcus crucis: see leg, open sore

Ulcus ventriculi et doudeni: see intestinal infection

Underweight: 32

Urethritis: as cystitis

Vegetative dystony: Melbrosia Executive 36

Vaginitis: insert propolis vaginal suppositories or tampons saturated with Melbrosia-propolis elixir 46, 59

Veins: varicose, spread on Salvacol-Cream lightly 54

Women's complaints: 19 onward, 22 onward, 59